Table of Contents

> "A failure to act is an act unto itself."
> My dear f riend, John Hill

ACKNOWLEDGEMENTS

I have many people to thank for influencing or helping me in some way or another to write these papers and letters. First, there are the people who showed me things about my computer such as Mimi Rivkin (I'm compelled to mention that during WWII she served in the CBI, the China, Burma, India Theater), Neal (Fergie) Ferguson, Jack Bean, Roberta Spangler, and Grace Turner, Benita Smith and C. Todd Chessmore.

There was Maj. Gen. Richard M. Lee, who made me his enlisted aide in the U.S. Army and taught me a great deal of what I know about the world we live in. When I mentioned to him some forty years ago that I was thinking about writing a book addressing my opinion on what isn't being done in Black America by Black leaders, he urged me to do so. However, I thought it too controversial at that time and declined.

Then there is the family that I was born into. My father, Theodore Roosevelt Wilson, Sr., started teaching me responsibility by the time I was about three (I remember him telling me that I could go to town with him the next day if I woke up on my own) and continued to do so until he died. He died before I turned seven years old. My mother, Effie Dora Garrard Wilson, did her best to teach me manners and to try to get along with people in this world (it could be said

—

that she failed somewhat on the former). My sisters, Loretta Johnson and Ernestine Wilson, and my other siblings who have since passed away: Dorothy Betton, Ruby Lois Holloway, Mildred Harris, and the gentlest of them all, Beulah White, who have always done everything they could to make me feel that I was an important person. One of them told me on her death bed how they enjoyed spoiling me. I never guessed that I was spoiled, never!

Although I have no knowledge of having any biological children, I do have five "children." They are Colin Minter, Virginia Parker, Linda Ottey, Brenda McNeil, and Michael Standback. These children tell me that I'm a good father, and I try to be. They fill a very empty space in my life and I shall thank them eternally.

I want to thank my sister, Loretta, for her tireless search for effective treatments for some of my senior ailments. And I have to issue a special thanks to my sister, Ernestine, who was kind enough to edit this book for me such as I would let her, and to my other editor, Caren Burmeister.

DEDICATION

This book is dedicated to the memory of

STEVE BIKO

Steve Biko is a South African Black man who was brutally tortured and murdered by the South African apartheid police. Biko's crime, as those Christian police saw it, was that he wanted Black South African people to take responsibility for their well-being and think in terms of something called "Black Consciousness." Here in America, I have not heard Biko's name mentioned by any politician, any news organization, nor any Black leader for approximately the last two generations. But I have thought of Biko often and believe that Black Americans would do well to adopt the general goals he sought for Black South Africans. This is not to say that America is an apartheid nation, or that White Americans collectively have attitudes similar to those of apartheid White South Africans.

This book is about what Black Americans should do. It's not about expecting something of White Americans except that they behave like Americans.

Steve Biko wanted Black South Africans to think of something called "Black Consciousness." I want Black Americans to consider "Black Awareness and Responsibility."

7

That would mean that in every Black community in this nation, people would know that whatever values their children hold, raising young people are the responsibility of the local community, not the city councils, mayors, governors, the U. S. Congress or the President of the United States.

If assistance can be obtained from any of these elements, it should be requested and readily accepted. These responsibilities, however, are solely that of communities. So, when our young men continue to kill each other with the same abandon that people usually reserve for dangerous poisonous snakes or rabid dogs, something should be done about it. Something should have been done about it long ago. As stated elsewhere, when someone has tried to do something about it previously, they have failed miserably. I count myself as among those who failed by thinking I was not important enough to speak out. Others, I'm sure, have their excuses, but what is desperately needed is results, not excuses.

Forty-nine years ago, when George Wallace ran for president, he said that if elected, the streets of Washington, D.C. would be safe, even if he had to post National Guard soldiers every ten feet along the streets. If posting soldiers is what it takes to stop our young people from killing each other, then goddamnit, do it!

Of course, I never met Biko, but I believe that were he to address Black Americans today, he would be saying essentially the same thing.

It should be noted that Ted Wilson served fourteen years and seven months in the U.S. Air Force, achieving the rank of staff sergeant before he was honorably discharged. He then entered the U.S. Army, where he served nearly nine years before retiring as a sergeant first class.

Ted Wilson in 1951, when he was stationed at Hamilton Air Force Base near San Francisco.

Ted Wilson was a member of the Honor Guard at
Pease Air Force Base in Portsmouth, New Hampshire
in 1957.

Ted Wilson in 1966 at II Corps Headquarters
in Pleiku, Vietnam with friend, Tech Sgt.
Hazzard.

Ted Wilson was an enlisted aide to Maj. Gen. Richard M. Lee at U.S. Forces Japan headquarters at Fuchu Air Station in Tokyo in 1972.

Ted Wilson, left, receiving the Army Commendation Medal from Army Maj. Gen. Richard M. Lee in Fuchu, Japan.

FORWARD

I imagine some will wonder what and where this book, such as it is, comes from. As you read it, you will easily conclude that parts of it are letters I wrote to someone; others will say a lot less about the sources.

In the early 1970s, I wrote letters to my godchildren or other minor family members – truly concerned about how they would grow up in a world such as it was. Toward the end of that decade, I wrote the paper addressed to a young American. A friend who read the paper kept referring to it as my book and asked when I going to finish it. However, another person didn't like it at all. He indicated that he would prefer never to see it as a finished book. Being a person who does not like to offend people, and seeing that he was offended by the paper, I decided not to continue writing on the subject of Black America. Years later, (I am eighty-five years old as I write these words in the year of our Lord 2017) I wrote the paper called "Mothers Who Have Lost Children To Violence" out of frustration with the direction some young Black people are taking.

Earlier this year when I showed my friend, Benita Smith, one of the godchildren letters, she said, "Ted, you ought to publish this." Later, when I gave copies of Letter to a Young American Person and another paper to Dr. Herman Green and his co-worker,

14

Purvis Thurman, they insisted I turn them into a book. It was then that I decided to do so.

Certainly, some will disagree with what I say and condemn it. Had I been writing for the general public, I am not sure I would have said some of these things or used the same tone. What I can say is this: these were my true thoughts expressed to the best of my ability as I wrote them. I was not writing for the general public, but for family members and my godchildren. So, in some sections, you will be reading their mail.

In the last part of this book, I did write for public consumption. Should a reader disagree, I hope they have the ability to take up pen and express their disagreement. My opinion is that there are some things that need to be said, and if no one else is saying them, I have the responsibility to say them myself.

LETTER TO MY GODCHILDREN, 1972

In the early 1970s I became concerned about the world and wrote letters to my six godchildren attempting to inform them of the dangers of accepting bad ideas.

My dear godchildren,

I hope you are all fine as you receive this letter. Now that the holiday season is over, I suppose we should all go back to the business of living our everyday lives. Those of you in upstate New York are probably enjoying the heavy winter snow while the others in California are being deluged with rain. I have spent winters in both places, and frankly, I am not particularly fond of either type of weather. But most people do like them, especially snow, and I hope that all of you are enjoying the weather where you are.

The weather here in Tokyo, where I am now living, has winters with both rain and snow: It rains often and seldom snows. I said that I didn't like either kind of weather, but I certainly don't hold an extreme dislike for any kind of weather.

Incidentally, I hope all of you will save this letter and refer to it in the future. Maybe some of you don't understand what I'm trying to say now and will be able to do so as you grow older. On the other hand, since I'm fully convinced of what I'm saying, this might just serve to show just how wrong a person can be – so save it. It is guaranteed for future use.

My intention in writing this letter is to let you know about some of the problems I think you will probably face in your lives. I want you to know what they are like and my opinion of how to behave if you have these problems.

If I tell you anything that is different from what your parents have told you, or differs from what they tell you later, then your parents are right, and I am wrong. You see, your parents are responsible for your well-being in all respects, while I'm just working at it part-time. So, the privilege of having the last word belongs to the parent. Remember that; parents have the final say whether they are talking to their children or any other person on matters concerning their children. But let's go on.

I have mentioned dislikes. There are different kinds of people and they will dislike different kinds of things. People should be free to like or dislike whatever they choose, but an ignorant person might expect that everyone should like whatever he likes. This does not necessarily mean he should be condemned because he is ignorant. However, being ignorant in matters he should know about does leave him open to severe criticism. The reason I dislike ignorance in a person is that he is liable to behave neither sensibly nor honorably when the chips are down. He is most apt to

17

act maliciously. Maliciousness is when a person does something mean to another person, often when that person has not done anything mean to him. This brings us to racism and racists.

Racism is when a person's attitude in which he thinks his race is better than any other and is thus entitled to special privileges. A person who practices racism is called a racist. America once had a lot of White racists. Now it has many, both Black and White. The White racists did a lot of evil in the past and they're still doing it. The Black racists are doing just as much evil if not more, but we haven't seen the end result of their racism yet. The Black racists would call their racism pride and consider it good, while calling White racism bad and calling it prejudice. It is all very bad. Throughout time, people have managed to do bad things and call it good, to give their badness a good name.

It is said that there is a great deal of good in the Black awareness program. If someone is to say that it is not, let it not be me. But let me hasten to add that the world has not found a sincere need for the person who makes a career of being Black. There is a demand for a variety of people, including doctors and dog catchers; professors, pawnbrokers and priests; songwriters, soldiers, scientists and swimmers; musicians, missionaries, mechanics and mathematicians; ecologists and several kinds of missionaries. This just

18

starts the list, but a person's color, race, creed, religion or ethnic group is important only to the most narrow-minded thinker.

In practical cases, a person is identified by his or her talent, skill or profession, not his color. People ask themselves: What can this person do that is useful? He isn't doing anyone much good and might be doing a lot of bad if his main contribution is yelling that he is "Black" and "proud." Proud? Proud of what? Being Black is nothing more than a biological accident. It is yet centuries away, but some day all the people of the world will probably be shades of brown. In the future, a totally Black or totally White person might run the risk of being put in the zoo on public display.

Pride is a feeling of well-being and confidence usually brought about by a personal accomplishment. A person might be proud of getting all A's on his report card or running faster than anyone in school, but he would not properly be proud of being black. If, however, a person is indeed proud, he or she need never say it (that includes those claiming to be proud to be a Texan. Nobody cares.) His or her way of doing things would show that they were proud. Being proud is not a declaration, and the fact that someone goes around yelling that he is proud might mean that he is not that at all, but is too slow to know it.

Aside from occasionally having known certain beautiful ladies here and there who knew how to behave beautifully, being Black is about the most unimportant thing that has happened to me. Surely, we suffer hardships and get our feeling hurt sometimes. We could have all died when we were babies. Should anyone be ugly toward you solely because you are Black, you should recognize him or her as an ignorant, insecure person who is trying to raise themselves up by putting you down.

Now, one final thought before we go on. A fellow told me a few days ago that he was first and foremost a Black man. This raises a question. If a Brown, White or Yellow man is identified as an architect, a lawyer, or by some other profession, why would a Black man want to be known as a Black man first and his profession second. In this case, the Black man seems to be insisting he is different, which then might require that he be treated differently. This will almost certainly result in bad treatment, not good treatment, especially, since it will probably be coming from non-Blacks.

Everything I'm saying might be different from what you hear every day from your friends, although I hope it is not. But it is alright with me if it is. I am an individualist and do not feel obligated to think what everyone else thinks, or say what others say. An individualist is a person who thinks for him or herself. Some people can think for themselves, but don't have the courage to voice an opinion that is contrary to other widely-held opinions. So, I would urge all of you to think, and think, and think. People can always tell you to do, or not do, something. But you alone can control your thinking. If you are going to think well, you are going to have to know a number of things. This is another reason why it is so important to learn all you can while you're in school and to continue reading books after you get out.

It's also imperative for the person who would succeed to pursue things on his own initiative. Many people who are rich today started out poor, but had the drive, knowledge, and will power to get rich. And many of their children will die poor because they didn't have the drive to do anything except spend money and get into trouble. I have seen people willing to stand idle and watch while someone died just because they did not trust themselves to act, indicating that someone had always acted for them. So, if you are not in the habit of washing dishes and cleaning your room, start doing so now and start doing it without having to be told.

Another question: What do you do in a bad situation? It's easy to be a good child if everything is fine and you have all the goodies you want. But what do you do when you don't have them? Do you cry and make everyone around you unhappy? Do you make a bad situation worse? That's what a lot of people do.

They make a bad situation worse. It is not what I want you to do.

People are more likeable when they convey the message that they mean no harm to their fellow man. We often see athletes, especially boxers, shaking hands after a fierce competition. This is their way of saying they meant each other no harm and the competition was friendly. It is always better to function in an atmosphere of friendliness and cooperation, regardless of what is being accomplished. The obligation to create this atmosphere is placed equally on all persons involved, when everyone involved is equal.

Whenever something goes wrong, I want you to write me and tell me about it, and I will write an answer back to you. I wish I could be there to see you and talk to you. That way, I could avoid having to write you these long, long letters. It would pain me deeply if I were to learn that one of you had gone wrong or felt bad because of something I had failed to do. I have the highest hopes for each of you. Should you not make something of yourselves, it will be as much my fault as anyone else's. I don't think anyone has ever felt a stronger responsibility than what I feel regarding your well-being.

I want to hear from all of you, so write. I remain,

Your hopeful godfather,

Ted Wilson

LETTER TO GODCHILDREN 1974

Hi Kids,

I imagine you might have wondered what had happened to me having heard nothing of any consequence from your godfather lately. Actually, a lot has happened to me. My reasons for not writing before are many. I lean heavily on the facts of my inability to form coherent sentences and that I thought myself too busy. Then, too, it is this: I do not intend to interrupt your youthful innocence again with these serious thoughts except on a "requested" or an "as needed" basis.

Hollywood has recently given Godfathers a bad name. Consequently, Maybe I can be forgiven for blundering here and there. Things like blunder flavor life. One is more apt to keep his guard up knowing the he might err.

My intention was to write you another letter soon after the last, which was intended to be an interim measure. The two-year delay is a result of the composition problem. My sudden decision to write now came from two sources. One was the recent war in the Middle East. What would happen, I thought, if I go off to war and get myself killed. Will anyone ever say the specific things that I believe need to be said so badly. The fact that it might be left to someone else when I could do it myself was disturbing.

Those were my thoughts. My concern was not that I might die but that I might die and leave something undone. My opinion is that it does not become a man to be functionally afraid of anything at all. I, however, am afraid of death. Should you learn that I died in the process of bringing war to some distant people, spare me your tears. If you insist on crying for me, cry because I no longer live the life I love. Spend your real sorrow on the parents (mine if you chose) who lose their sons in the "ultimate game," of war. Grieve for the innocents who suffer the agonies of war, those who offer violence to none and can have no understanding of why a war is happening to them. But rather than crying for me, I would rather you and your best friend go out and have some ice cream together.

In the letter two years ago, we talked about the obstacles you might encounter in your lives as Black Americans. Actually, they are not that different from the same basic problems you might expect to have if you were of any other race in any other country (millions of people around the world wish their problems were just twice those of the worst-off Americans). I find my previous contentions more pertinent today and only hope to express the ideas better this time.

My reluctance in writing this letter lies in knowing that I do so at the risk of becoming a bore. Surely this is the kind of things your parents say to you all the time. If we differ refer to your last letter. If we agree and seem to be conspiring, we are. We are conspiring to help you become a good student, a good person, a happy person, and ultimately a competent person. We are conspiring to help you become a person who is on acceptable terms with himself and his world. We are conspiring because we are concerned about your social and academic development. We are conspiring because we know that anything we fail to do at a given time cannot be corrected a few years later. Most of all, we are conspiring because you are an extension of us, and we succeed or fail as you succeed or fail.

I hear much frightful talk these days about the poor quality of life in the ghetto. What is a ghetto? A few years ago (less than twenty), a ghetto was a special kind of community in European cities inhabited by Jews, or Hebrews. These communities were of themselves rather indistinct in character. Today, the ghetto is an American phenomenon. When people say ghetto, they refer to a place with a very distinct character, a place inhabited by Blacks encompassing practically all aspects of the human condition that is considered bad. Overlooking the rhetoric and questionable definition, the ghetto is just a piece of innocent geography. But the ghetto is distinguished from its surrounding neighborhoods by its residents' values and actions. All the bussing and assistance in the world will not change the existing conditions in the ghettos without a major effort on the part of the ghetto dwellers themselves. This truism always seems to get lost in the translation when people speculate on why conditions are the way they are. Somehow, no one ever manages to say that this is what has to be done and this is how we are going to do it.

Instead they prefer to dwell on the immense superiority of our African Heritage. Complex problems like the conditions in Black American Ghettos are not going to be solved by that kind of thinking. I don't think anyone qualified to address the subject questions our heritage, or that great civilizations once flourished there, or that African kings ruled millions. So what? Does it justify some of the current fads being offered as African culture? I doubt very much that any civilized African culture has adult males wearing braided hair. Somehow, it seems more conjecture, or a cultural rip off, than a cultural tradition.

History itself is nothing more than the quasi-official record of man's effort to subject his neighbor. Unable to do that, he subjected his brother. Look at the Chinese, for example. They have killed some fifty million (my estimate) of their own in assorted civil wars over the past one hundred and thirty years or so.

Africa had Nigeria five years ago. Black, Brown, Red, and Yellow racists would do themselves credit by saying, "Welcome to the club, Whitey, we realize you got here with the rest of us. You rated in a class of your own. Your excellence in violence and destruction is commendable yet condemnable, but welcome. We give the devil his due."

That which makes one man a bad person also makes the next man a bad person. The world does not have one standard for a Japanese person, another for an Indian person and yet another for a Canadian person. If greed makes a European person bad, greed also makes a South American person bad. If racial prejudice makes a White person bad, it also finds some of the half-tended braided hair the most unsightly feature in civilized dress I have ever encountered in my travel on four continents, including Africa.

Unblushingly, your honor, I stand

Before you and do not feel the need to

Lower my eyes as I am an American. My ancestors were

brought to this land in chains, which they wore for some

Two hundred and fifty years. When the chains were removed, they could not

Return to their native land so they

Stayed here and became citizens with

All the privileges and responsibilities of all other

citizens. Africa?

Africa, your honor, was the home of my distant

ancestors.

My home is here. My presence here today as a man and

a citizen is more important than the chronologies of

thousands of African kings. I have a future.

Individual people are not equally endowed. Some are taller, and some are smarter, and some are faster, and some are prettier, and some are stronger, and some are meaner. Name it and someone has more of it. The unequal distribution of natural attributes is often what determines which of us will excel in the various fields. An especially talented person might excel without putting forth his best effort; however, those who most often excel are those who tend to apply themselves diligently to the task at hand.

The area of academics is especially demanding of the time of those who pursue it. You can command the praise and respect of your teachers and classmates now by completely learning your school assignments. By continuing at that pace, you can earn the respect of the world later on in life. On the other hand, you'll probably fail if you are just doing enough to get by. When I was your age, a great many people tried to make me see the need to get an education, but they just couldn't reach me. Since then, I have had numerous occasions to curse the chance that was wasted. People often do that. You too will be cursing the chance that was wasted as you look back in hindsight wishing you had done better in school, and later on wishing you had done better in life. The time to keep all that from happening is now. It will be too late all too soon.

If I was in a position to demand anything of any of you, I would demand that you apply yourselves academically to the best of your abilities. I would ask you to do extra assignments to help you understand how you and the area where you live affect others. I wish I could personally take you back to some of the places I've been and show you some of the mistakes that I and others have made.

The successful person in life is one who can correctly interpret his situation and adjust his behavior accordingly. The person who is a successful student today will be a successful doctor, engineer, or pilot tomorrow. You will find later in life that people will go back to your school records to see what kind of student you were. So, realize that you are already making a name for yourself. I hope that it is good name, as a good name is an indication of a good person.

A good person will resist the temptation to be anything else. A good person will always do his best in whatever he attempts. People might realize that he's not the brightest, nor the most likable, nor the most even tempered. But if he is a good person, no one will doubt it. Being good means no one could truthfully say he was unfair in anything. No one could say he let someone execute a responsibility that he knew to be his own. He would know that, as it is written, "There is a time for everything." He would surely take a risk before he asked someone else to take it. He would hold the conviction that anytime his destiny was not in the hand of his God, it was in his own hands. Finally, a good person would always be prepared to face their detractors and unashamedly account for his actions.

Those of you who reach these standards are going to be resented by your classmates. Those very same friends who liked you very much when you got a "D" in gym and they got a "B" will sometimes resent it when you get an "A" in mathematics and they get a "B." Envy is the curse of those who excel. You will have to learn some tact and diplomacy. Any fool could tell the envious person that the reason they didn't get a good grade was because they didn't study, but how many would have the grace to show the envious person that he still thought him worthy? Approach him or her in a friendly manner and say that their failure to excel does not detract from your friendship, if you have one. You might be hated for life if you act superior when you excel at something and act superior.

Show that envious person some tolerance and understand that this is the kind of thing the strong and the great have always done for the weak and the damned. Whatever you decide to do, do it with taste, and do it with style.

I urge you to strive to make something of yourselves other than just other citizens. Set a reasonable goal for yourselves and never, ever accept anything less until you no longer seek that particular goal, or until it is no longer within your reach.

There are two good reasons why you should always listen to your parents. One is that they always have your best interest at heart. The other is, they are responsible for you.

There is no help available from any source on earth that will equal what you can give yourself. I urge you to think for yourselves, and I want you to feel free to believe, or not believe, anything or any idea expressed in this letter.

On the other hand, you should not employ any aspect of this letter if you know that your parents do not approve of it. Read the letter carefully and ask mom or dad to explain anything you do not fully understand. If you want my view on anything, ask your parents and then ask me, and it will be forthcoming.

All of you will find $5 in this letter. I want you to check with your parents and go out and buy all the hamburgers, ice cream and sodas you want. Because as I recall, nothing is more pleasant than to be young and able to get all the goodies you want at a given time.

Cheers,

Godfather

LETTER TO AN AMERICAN YOUNG PERSON

Around 1980 I became very concerned about what was going on in my community. I held the opinion that there was very little I could about it.

I had read somewhere that President Abraham Lincoln had a disagreement with someone. He had written a letter expressing his discontent but declined to forward it to that person. Instead, he kept the letter in his desk drawer. I wrote a paper expressing what I thought were the problems in our community. After showing the letter to some of the people I knew, I did nothing else with it.

....

Somewhere along the way to the last quarter of the twentieth century, a dreadful thing happened to Black America. In its attempt to achieve the American promise in its entirety, Black America lost perspective of its responsibility in the process. Consequently, the present prospect is that of pending failure — failure of a people to reach some very attainable goals. While these goals are sought under conditions that are less than ideal, they most certainly can be reached. When this failure is documented in history, it will most appropriately be laid at the feet of those — some very well intentioned — who occupy positions of leadership in Black America.

And Black America. What is it? Is it a faction of the socio-political entity that is the United States of America? Is it a society within a society? Or, is it an integral part of the U.S. that more or less sleeps separately. Surely it is to some extent all of those things, but perhaps it is more accurately described by the latter.

For it is there, concentrated in some of the nation's most congested urban quarters – Harlem, Watts, Chicago's Southside, the Southeast quadrant of Washington, D.C., East Baltimore, and San Francisco's Fillmore District – that the quality of life for millions of Blacks differs significantly.

By day, a great many partake in what economist John Kenneth Galbraith referred to in his 1958 book, The Affluent Society. By night, they move back to what I am now moved to call "the fortified society," also known as the Black ghettos that developed in the following decades. Fortified? Yes, and fortified it had very well better be.

The prudent thing to do in urban America is to lock it up. Lock the door when you leave the house. Lock the door when you are in the house. Answer the door and keep it locked with a chain until you have identified the caller. Lock the door with a minimum of three locks, too, and don't consider it excessive to lock with six locks. Lock the car when you get into it. Lock the car when you get out of it, even if you don't expect to be out of it for more than two minutes.

Lock the car with locks that cannot be opened from the outside with a coat hanger. After having locked everything, then alarm everything because the thieves might break through all those locks and the system will announce their presence. Also, should the alarm go off, there is a possibility that a neighbor will hear the alarm and make an effort to protect you or your property, if you are not at home.

Hopefully, that concerned neighbor will not endanger his life, as life is relatively cheap in modern Black America. And life can be exceedingly cheap in modern Black America should one attempt the absolute indiscretion of attempting to impede an armed criminal who is in pursuit of his chosen life style. Of course, life is cheap in Black America. So many things have evolved to make it so. It seems that assorted people with varied interests have unwittingly conspired over more than three-and-a-half centuries to create the optimum atmosphere. First, it was the slave traders who killed to let free men know that those among them who were not killed would henceforth be slaves.

Quickly following was the slave owners and overseers who killed and maimed to maintain control of the peculiar institution. Then, after the Civil War, it was the disenfranchised Southern White man killing to regain his diminished authority and to protect the virtue of his White woman or, possibly worse, his Black woman. Presently, it is some of those who would have been Black leaders — had they availed themselves of the opportunity — conveying to highly impressionable young Black men the idea that certain lawless conduct is both understood and condoned should one conclude that society is not fulfilling their needs. Naturally the most pressing need, as it has always been understood to be, is money. Thus, these young Black people turn to crimes of profit.

The easiest and closest victims of these crimes are the criminal's neighbors, other Blacks. What is being described here contributes more toward the poor quality of life in the so-called Black ghettos than any other single factor. No discussion of the quality of life in Black America could be adequately undertaken without seriously reflecting on the taking of human life. Taking a human life in Black America has come easy. A decade ago, the National Violence Commission released a statistic that in eleven of twelve cases of homicide in America, it was one Black taking the life of another Black. Some Blacks will deny the accuracy of that statistic, while others will say - and quite honestly believe - that there is a good reason for it. They will cite such vague causes as black frustration and deprivation.

Of course, people are, have been, and are going to be unhappy. But the record should show that there is at least one Black man in the republic who is just as unenthusiastic about being murdered by a frustrated Black as he is about being killed by a racist White.

Not wanting to be murdered is the kind of thing that one would ordinarily do something about. He would know not to wait until after, say, two members of his family had been murdered to start thinking that something should be done about murderers. In a country where there seems to be an ever-increasing number of murders, it would be appropriate if the capital punishment alternative was under serious consideration in every state.

Every society should take means to protect itself from criminals of every bent. It would seem that any entity could devise a means to protect itself from any perceived real threat, even if the perceived threat is its own prevailing values.

In fact, Black America, to its peril, has ignored values and embraced money all too often. Consequently, we see our young requesting $80 sneakers and such. The problem could possibly be solved by a respected adult explaining that with $6 shoes or $100 shoes, who he or she is will be determined by their usefulness to society, their conduct toward their fellow man and their general deportment. If, however, an adult doesn't know it, he can hardly teach it. Black America collectively has been too concerned about money and other tangibles. This is not to say that they aren't important, but only important in perspective.

Black Americans financial circumstance is much better than it is for most all lower-income groups in many foreign countries. It is mostly by comparison with other Americans that some Black Americans tend to fall behind in maintaining the higher standard of living. Most ethnic groups in America seem to collectively fall into higher income groups than Black Americans.

However, numerous examples do exist of communities upon communities of very affluent Black Americans, especially in the urban areas of the country. But still, the percent of Black Americans earning those incomes falls below that of their White counterparts.

One aspect of the income problem is America's labor structure. Politically, an excellent friend of Black America, organized labor has nonetheless contributed significantly to Black America's financial woes. Organized labor demands and receives higher wages for its members. But with fewer Blacks belonging to the unions, the income gap between the races widens each year, and Blacks and other low-paid groups fall further and further behind. Thus, a barely tolerable situation threatens to become wholly intolerable in the coming years.

Many Americans thought integration was the solution to the problem. They were wrong about that, and many other things, too. Integration is in as much trouble now as it was a generation ago (in the 1950s) although from a different source. After emancipation, Black Americans tried for a full century to break the barriers that kept them out of White institutions, especially White universities. Finally, well into the third quarter of the twentieth century, those efforts were rewarded. Not only were qualified Blacks permitted into those pockets of White exclusivity, some not so very qualified Blacks were also permitted to enroll. Good!

Whites, with a long history of what seemed to be a collective insensitivity to the aspirations of Blacks, were finally showing some compassion and understanding, responses that were notably unreciprocated as it turned out.

No sooner had Black students gotten themselves established in these mostly all-White campuses that they requested, not complete integration, but another form of segregation. This was the Black student unions, Black newspapers and other activities established exclusively Black and identified accordingly. Tastelessness is the very best that can be ascribed to these actions.

Why an all-Black anything in the middle of a White institution? The answer was, "To show them that we can have something nice, too." That thought is indescribably fallacious. Whatever Black America has, nice or otherwise, White America knows about it. Just as it knows about whatever Black Africa or White Europe does or does not have (the White man's sins are many and varied, but collective stupidity is not one of them). As a result, an attempt to impress was wasted and an opportunity was lost. This loss was the opportunity for genuine friendship and social intercourse.

Notwithstanding being credited with god-like attributes by some Blacks, the White person is quite mortal. However subtle their response to slights or embarrassments, it is liable to be all too mortal. So, when the Black student leaves the exclusively Black function expecting to greet his White counterpart as an equal, the White person could be thinking something quite different.

The White person could be thinking, "We are not equals, you and I. This inequality was established when you excluded me from your all-Black function, the very kind of thing you have insisted I not do. I would have liked you more had you not done this. Now, I do not know which of us is superior and which is inferior, nor do I know what makes it so, but this kind of thing does not transpire between two equals!"

This suggestion that some Blacks have mental images of Whites as god-like will be met with prompt denials. It is, however, sometimes true. It is possible that centuries of involuntary servitude surface in this manner. One example of Whites being assessed with godly attributes is a song by a famous Black vocal group. One line goes, "Heaven help the White man if he fails to hear us pray." Hear us pray? Pray! One does not pray to his neighbor or antagonist, he prays to his God. No one thinks that a mortal could hear a prayer, not in this context. Hearing prayers is the divine province of the gods of all religions.

This, as stated, is not only a bad song, but it has something to do with mindset, just as most songs have something to do with mindset. Moreover, it is just one of many equally bad songs. Possibly one of the worst of songs is one about an unfortunate soul escaping life's hard knocks by using drugs. The idea is presented straight forward. Words lament the circumstance of the person's existence but escape from the reality is achieved through the use of drugs. After the fix, the person is "f-e-e-e-e-e-e-l-i-n-g fine." We will never see a better endorsement of drug use. Surely some authority in a population of about two hundred and fifty million people must have recognized the potential consequence of that song and felt the need to condemn it. No one did.

Many children, particularly children from families with low incomes, certainly related to that song. Some probably heard the song and felt it was written just for them. We will never know how many children were persuaded that, yes, drug use is not that bad after all. But we do know that, as the song played in America in the mid-1960s, drug use skyrocketed. The song was pretty. It had rhythm, was nicely arranged, and had all the aspects of an excellent song except that it conveyed such a bad idea. An idea which adversely affected the quality of life in Black America and ultimately may have contributed to the ruin of this nation.

That song, along with the Vietnam War and Timothy O'Leary urging young people to, "Turn on, tune in and drop out," resulted in a lot of national heartache and pain.

The future of nations is determined by the kind of investments those nations make in their children. In those days, I was obsessed with the idea that White America was alienating its children with its corruption, while Black America was corrupting its children with its alienation. I am still convinced, except those children are grown now and some of them are both corrupt and alienated.

Not surprisingly, alienation flourishes in Black America. Alienation gave birth to the tragedy that was Jonestown.

Jonestown is a study in alienation and ignorance. What could provoke hundreds of people, mostly Black, to abandon home, family, and friends to go off into an unknown alien wilderness? The hope of going to Russia? No. They were not so much going somewhere as they were leaving somewhere — the shores of America.

If we could recall those people from the dead, and get a consensus of their thinking, we could learn something about complete disappointment. We would probably learn there was more to what triggered Jonestown than just a perverse Christianity that finally lost balance and fell in the wrong direction. But, more than nine hundred people did fall, most of them alienated victims of Vietnam, Watergate, and racism, many of them Blacks leaving America but not returning to Africa.

Had the good Reverend organized properly, his following could well have been ninety thousand, all believers alienated to the extent that were venturing into a strange land with a language in which most could not even say hello.

A millionaire would not long remain rich if he were passing out one hundred-dollar bills in exchange for quarters.

Everyone has to do the math to determine where they are headed. And I'm not just talking about simple arithmetic. I'm talking about looking to see where certain activities will take us. For instance, what does a habit of casual, unprotected sex equal? AIDS. What is the sum total of an under-educated adult? Most often it is low income jobs. What is the total of young men, guns, and almost any disagreement? Shooting and killing. What do we get if we add up drugs, money, guns, and territorial disputes? Murder, murder and more murder. Americans need to start doing the math and put forth every conceivable effort to insure our children learn to do the same.

(This is a modified version of my original 1979-80 paper)

Ted Wilson

LETTER TO MOTHERS WHO HAVE LOST THEIR CHILDREN TO VIOLENCE

Had my mother, a Black woman, lived until her next birthday, she would have been one hundred years old. It is in her honor that I dare to suggest that I have an offering on a subject dear and painful to women such as my mother. But I do dare, and I'm ashamed to see how the violence in our communities has escalated in the last three decades and that I didn't say something like this long ago.

Nothing in the following lines should be construed to mean that I propose to be talking only to Black mothers or, for that matter, only to Black people. Not so long ago, I was struck by a local news story about mothers who had lost children to violence. They were having a meeting that welcomed only those who had suffered that devastating tragedy. It was easy to understand their need to share their pain only with others who had undergone a similar experience. I thought, however, that they might have had another gathering where others participated. I flattered myself that I might have a contribution, however slight, toward a solution to this recurring nightmare.

Because, notwithstanding any apparent disconnect I have with those mothers, I share their pain and hurt with every news story, and the news stories

45

are endless. And while my pain was probably much less intense than those grieving parents, it has lingered and constantly renewed itself for three excruciating decades.

Any casual observer can see we are presently without a solution. If we have reached that conclusion, then we must have this question. Why?

How can it be that a newborn baby comes into our community like a blank sheet of paper on which we may write anything we so desire. Then we, with all our good intentions (paving the road to hell, no less) all too often turn him into a criminal or a murderer by the time he is fifteen years old? Moreover, we have of late managed to endow our young women with some of these same undesirable attributes.

Something is very much amiss. The time is long past when someone should have offered a workable solution to this problem. But in a phrase, "no such luck." What we have been presented with is an array of "cop outs." It's racism, it's poverty, it's anything but a culture gone amok. But the fact is, that is what it is — a culture gone amok.

Events contributing to this deplorable state of affairs didn't happen overnight, nor two generations ago (an era which I will have something to say a lot about later). I think it really started happening four generations ago, when Black people from the South started voting with their feet.

Undereducated, self-conscious rural people from states like Alabama, Georgia, and Mississippi were not, in an effective way, prepared for the social and psychological dynamics of living in urban cities like New York, Detroit, and Los Angeles. Consequently, when they moved to one of these "oasis of freedom," they often ignored their own values. And if they didn't adopt, then they at least accepted those in their new communities. Probably a great many of them had never exercised the courage of their convictions, making them exceedingly prone to accepting the values of what they considered to be sophisticated city folk.

These city folks were quick to look down their noses at the newcomers and did not hesitate to remind them that they were no longer "down South," adding to the newcomers' sense of social inadequacy.

This is not to say that Northern Blacks had a lot to offer in the way of enhancing the lives of Southerners of their race. Aside from a culturally acquired ability to enunciate the R's in the king's English, they had mostly nothing at all to offer.

In some cities (Washington, D.C. and Baltimore come to mind), the educated tend to go out of their way to denigrate the existence of Blacks from the South. As late as September 2007, I was introduced to an elderly lady from Washington, D.C. who made a point of telling me that I wasn't from somewhere important. Her point was, "you're not as good as me."

My family migrated from Alabama in 1944 and eventually moved to Utica, New York. I've seen this kind of conduct have devastating effects on close family members. Having suffered discrimination by Whites from the cradle, this brought on a kind of "you too, Brutus" syndrome that did nothing for one's self-esteem. Self-esteem is at the core of the problem, in my opinion.

Let us fast forward from the 1930s and 1940s to two generations ago. Culturally, there was a lot going on in the world in the mid-1960s. America was escalating the war in Vietnam; Blacks were petitioning federal, state, and municipal governments for their civil rights; and they were rioting in the streets when they felt they weren't getting them. In China, Mao Zedong, Chairman of the Communist Party of China, launched the cultural revolution.

What Mao did, for the uninitiated, was give teenagers the run of China to do as they saw fit. In an effort to somehow repair Chinese society, Mao said, "Let a hundred flowers bloom." In the process of blooming, Chinese teenagers wreaked havoc on the country in the few succeeding years.

For his part, President Lyndon B. Johnson said he wanted to continue programs started by his successor. While telling his detractors, "Let's reach a consensus" and "I'll go any place at any time" to discuss peace, he vetoed recommended locations for those very talks and sent our B-52s over Hanoi and Haiphong.

What Black American leaders said, however unintentional, as clearly evidenced by what we see in our inner cities today, was, "Let millions of flowers wither on the stem." And for some four decades now, young Black urban dwellers have, as their Chinese counterparts did under Mao Zedong, brought violence, drugs, heartbreak, disappointment, death, and tears as they killed each other wholesale in an unending state of self-destruction in our communities (In the last 24 hours, news headlines read: Washington, D.C. Morns 15-year-old Murdered Over the Weekend; Delaware State College Suspends Student who Shot Two Others; University in Tennessee Investigates Murder of Football Player; and Overnight in Washington, D.C. 11 Shot, Four Fatally.)

In view of these statistics, how could anyone who professes to know anything not conclude that something is dreadfully wrong. Thirty-six-years ago, when I heard the words of Andrew Lloyd Webber's Jesus Christ Superstar, my mind immediately turned to Black American leaders:

"Every time I look at you I don't understand.
Why you let the things you did get so out of hand.

49

You'd manage better if you'd had a plan...."

But a plan was not what was most needed then, nor is it today. What is needed is understanding. When, and if, we understand, then we might find it an appropriate time to make plans. Something has made some young Black men the way they are today. We need to determine what it is and change it. Whatever it is, it has something to do with culture.

So, let's look at some incidents to demonstrate what I'm trying to get across.

Incident #1

About 20 years ago, I took my car to a garage and waited for it to be repaired. A woman who acted, I believe, as cashier, had her young seven-year-old son there. The child's grandfather and six other men worked in that garage. I don't believe I had been in the building more than twenty minutes before the boy's mother, grandfather, and four of the other men had described the boy as being "bad." I thought they grossly erred by describing the child that way but had no standing to tell them so.

However, I decided to do what I could to alleviate the situation and engaged the boy in conversation. After learning his name, I asked him if he were "bad." No response. I cajoled him: "Come on now, you really aren't "bad," are you? You're good, aren't you?" Still he refused to respond. I left him and started wandering around the garage looking for a certain kind of screw for my license plate.

Suddenly, I heard the kid say, "I'm gonna kill you." I looked up to see him standing before me with a long thin metal bar that he was holding like a spear. I then attempted to explain to him that it was wrong to kill someone and that it was not good to say it, even in playing. It was obvious that he was somehow impressed with me and wanted to be my friend. He had a tennis ball and a golf club and seemed to delight in asking me to hit the ball with the club.

We played our little game for some two hours or so. During that time, I could never, try as I might, get him to say that he would not kill me or that he was "good."

Obviously, that child's opinion of himself was something less than good. For functional purposes, his self-esteem was totally destroyed, as in the case of tens of thousands of other children in our community. Collectively, parents in our community tend to matter-of-factly introduce their children as being "bad." Whatever I think I know about the human condition, I do not think these comments are complimentary, and I don't think they are neutral. Therefore, I can only conclude they are critical statements, and that they are processed by the children as such. I further conclude

---

that what these children are learning "at their mother's knee," no less, is what a bothersome little nuisance they are. That adults are conveying the impression to these children that they have failed to meet accepted standards — whatever those standards happen to be — and that this impression is stated, confirmed, reinforced, and firmly implanted in the children's concept of self. While knowing they never intended any harm in any way, they conclude that they really are "bad."

As a result, their self-esteem is probably damaged to the extent that they conclude there is no benefit in obeying rules, being kind to others, obeying the laws, or conforming to any other norms that contribute to a harmonious society.

In my opinion, what these parents should be saying to their children is that they are good. Not only that they are good, but that there is no one in the world better than they are. And that no amount of wealth, power, or fame can in any way make anyone, be he king or anything else, better than they are. If we can get our children to believe that, it will make more of a difference than anything else in the world. But first, of course, we have to get the adults to believe it. That in itself will be a major undertaking.

Incident #2

A decade or so ago I read an interview with Tupac Shakur, a Black American rapper, poet, and actor. Apparently, he had experienced an incident with the law. What I detected was that it was his inclination not to do what he had done. Yet, he did it because he felt he had to do it to maintain his standing in the community.

The question before us is: what kind of a society do we live in that our young people do anti-social things to maintain what they think is expected of them?

Incident #3

Some of us will recall the story. A young black man from Baltimore was being arraigned in Atlanta. He overcomes his guard, takes his gun, kills three people and escapes. Somewhere in the night, he encounters a young White woman in the parking lot to her apartment complex and makes her take him into her house. During the ensuing hours, the woman convinces him that he is a better person than the one who committed his crimes and persuades him to give himself up to the police.

While the woman persuaded the young man that he was actually a better person than his very recent conduct indicated, his community in Baltimore failed to do that very thing in numerous ways and on many occasions. No, I do not know what these occasions were. But his values were formed, either by the community, or by its failure to shape his values constructively. It is a community's responsibility to instill values in its children, and children reflect the values they have learned. There is a term used by computer programmers, "garbage in, garbage out." The same applies to people as their personalities and characters are formed.

We have to find ways to favorably influence our children before they get into trouble. Some will recall the stories of Malcolm X and Eldridge Cleaver. Both of these men learned in prison what they didn't learn in their community. We could probably go back to those communities today and ask an ordinary citizen if the community failed those two individuals and get a resounding no! Yet those two men came out of prison as useful citizens, as opposed to what they were before they went in. This same result has been attained with tens of thousands of other young men.

However, all too many go to prison and get further indoctrinated into the criminal culture, many because of an inability to think for themselves. This takes us back to Tupac Shakur. What demon possessed him, and what demon possesses so many other young Americans who are inclined to disobey their finer instincts? The answer is culture, except in cases of mental deficiency, and it is suggested here that anyone who believes otherwise is probably in a state of delusion. Actually, these inclinations toward violence are induced daily by non-suspecting adults.

Telling children they are "bad" has already been discussed, but what does it mean to them when someone else is labeled as "bad?" We often hear adults discuss how someone was so "bad" they didn't let anyone "mess" with them. Way too often, adults teach their children not to "take" anything off anyone, just as they wouldn't take anything off anyone. Consequently, we find youngsters killing each other wholesale for no better reason that they believe themselves to have been "dissed." Having told a child that he or she is "bad," and then telling them what it is that "bad" people do, it is small wonder they find it appropriate to kill someone. Although it is ever so unintentional, children get taught to kill just as they get taught to read and write. But where did this teaching start?

Seventy years ago, as I started school in Alabama, the whipping was the solution to everything in our community. One of the most egregious crimes of all time in my estimation was the habit of whipping children because they had not learned something. This carried over to a whipping because a child forgot something or failed to do something. Men whipped their wives or beat them with their fists to maintain control. Then men attempted to control each other by threatening and beating them with their fists. That is the culture. This culture is what children learn and practice.

Fast forward to the last three decades. Suddenly, we have a territorial dispute. Opposing groups want to sell drugs in a given area. Along with these drugs come a lot of money and guns. Some guns are not ordinary guns, but rather military assault rifles. Lacking the social skills to negotiate these disputes, the understood solution is an act of murder. Whenever a murder is committed, someone becomes a murderer. All too often, these murderers are our teenage children. Before us now, staring us straight in the face is, what are we going to do about it. I sure hope you will find cause to do more than some friends I've talked with recently.

A few days ago, I spoke with one friend about this matter and today I spoke with two more. They all said there was nothing that we can do. While I have heard this many times before, I never expected to hear it from fellow military retirees. There is always something that can be done, and there are some things that must be done. This is one of them. We must stop our young people from murdering us and our children.

How can we do this? First, we must recognize and acknowledge that we have a problem. There are people watching TV and reading the newspapers every day who are unable to do that effectively. I have been told numerous times that White communities have as many, or more, murders than Black communities by people who really believe it. These are Black people who think so little of themselves that it has never occurred to them that they could behave better than White people. How thoughtless and sad.

Getting people to recognizing the problem is going to take some doing. But it is something that MUST BE DONE.

Why not conduct a series of studies? Why not send someone into neighborhoods to question children of all ages? Why not question children in various groups? Find out what they think and why they think it. Then track these children over time to learn their attitudes and determine how a five-year-old with an irresistible smile turned into a scowling sixteen-year-old looking forward to confronting someone.

I mentioned Mao Zedong and China a while back. Chinese people have traditionally looked on the rest of the people in the world as barbarians. Let us consider that a tendency of the human condition, as we most certainly know it doesn't apply to us. But before we dismiss the Chinese, let us do something. Let us adopt one of their useful philosophies, which is, "try not to make a bad situation worse than it already is." If we could start thinking like that it would stop a lot of the bleeding in our communities. Just think of how it would affect how we behave when we have a disagreement with someone. It is a solution within itself.

So, what else to do? Stop drug use. That is something that is probably more difficult than anything previously suggested here. America needs to do two things immediately about drug use: Initiate an accelerated education program about drug use and decriminalize it. That would be something for our think tank to study. But the insane practice that America has of putting drug users in jail for years on end is an idea straight from hell. Those who think we should put people in jail for drug use need to think again. Certainly, if we put one-fourth of America's drug users in jail today, the country could not function. Is there anyone here who doesn't know that? So, if we know that it is impossible to punish all drug users, why punish the few we so very selectively catch?

I'm one of those people who thinks he knows some things. One of those things is that if we could get people to stop telling children they are "bad" and start telling them they are good, we would have already made a major contribution toward the solution to this problem. Another thing we could do is write a new book of etiquette. I'm not suggesting circumventing

Emily Post and Amy Vanderbilt. This would be something produced solely for the development of childhood character. It would be not more than fifty easy to read pages, and it could be taught in school as a regular course, like music, one hour every two weeks.

This tangent I'm on is given rise by my feeling that something must be done. That's because our intellectuals have glaringly failed their responsibility to offer workable solutions to this problem. If I may, it is as if they didn't know (and I'm cleaning it up) a damned thing.

Some thirty or forty years ago, I read a work by W.E.B. DuBois called The Philadelphia Negro. From then until now I have not seen (not that I would have necessarily seen it if it existed) an appropriate work giving the guidance that is now so desperately needed in our communities. So, I do have one other suggestion. Someone needs to create a Black think tank. This think tank would look at our communities and determine what is causing some to behave the way they do and what is affecting their thinking. Then they would propose solutions. These solutions should not attribute our problems to racism. Racism has thrived in this country all along, and those who choose to practice it will always find reason. Racism is just a contributing actor posing as a usual suspect.

And don't give us another name. Since we have been African Americans for more than a decade now, some disoriented nomenclator has thought of some name we should start calling ourselves to solve these problems. Maybe we could go back to being Negroes, or Colored, or even Black (I liked being Black).

But don't do it.

....

I was struck by a comment by Ishmael Beah, who wrote A Long Way Gone: Memoirs of a Boy Soldier about how he was instructed to kill by being shown such things as Rambo movies. I read the book and learned about how their indoctrination was done and how it might relate to the violence in our communities. There was little. But I did find that Beah got his impression of New York City from rap music. He imagined it as a place where people shot each other on the streets without any social or legal consequences. Rather than walking, people rode around in sport cars going to nightclubs and looking for violence. Having been a child soldier in Africa, Beah was no longer interested in being in that kind of place because he had seen enough of that kind of activity back in Africa.

How can it be that we have not acknowledged how violent music and videos have instilled this same penchant for violence in the young Black people in America? Something has. Are we just too disengaged to see?

One last note. This think tank I'm suggesting does not necessarily need to be Black, nor for that matter be from this planet, but it needs to provide us with real, workable solutions to these problems.

Ted Wilson

October, 2007

A TREATISE ON WISDOM

(My response to a question from my eight-year old grand-niece)

Children, a question has been posed to me by none other than someone who has my own blood running through their veins. The question: Am I wiser, or do I possess more wisdom, than my sister because I am a few years older?

I will answer the question, but when I do it will be just one person's opinion. So, before I give my answer, I think I should say that some people have presumed that older people are wiser and able to think better than younger people.

We will start with Plato. Plato lived more than two thousand years ago and is considered to be one of the greatest thinkers of all time. Since Plato's death, people have constantly referred to what Plato thought about matters relating to the human condition and how human societies should live.

Plato imagined a society similar to America. In this society, a person had to be fifty years old before they could govern, or tell people how to behave and make laws. They also had to be trained to govern before they could govern. So, Plato thought that an older person was able to think better than a younger person or, as some would say, an older person was wiser than a younger person. So, along with Plato and just about every society here on earth, including Americans, people tend to think older people are wiser than younger people.

The American Constitution requires a person to be twenty-five years old before they can serve in the United States House of Representatives, a person must be at least thirty years old before they can serve in the United States Senate, and a person must be at least thirty-five years old before they may become the President of the United States. So, the idea that an older person is able to think better than a younger person is universal (meaning that it is what people think all over the world).

Most of us know, or think we know, that an eight-year-old probably knows more than a four-year-old. Or that a twelve-year-old probably knows more than an eight-year-old, and a twenty-five-year-old probably knows more than a twelve-year-old. All these things are probably true as it applies to general knowledge. But they are not necessarily true, especially when applied to specific knowledge. For instance, an eight-year-old knows exactly where he or she lives, but that child's teacher or the older kids in school probably do not. But generally, older people know more about the world we live in than younger ones.

By knowing more about our world, older people should know not to do stupid things. There are hundreds of stupid things that might be done, but high among them are driving a car too fast or unsafely, failing to fasten a seat belt, using drugs, or doing something that is extremely dangerous because some other kid dared them to do it or told them they were too scared to do it.

Life is a learning process from birth to death. Sometimes older people do not know more than younger people because they fail to continue learning. Some people stop reading books and newspapers when they get out of school. That doesn't mean they stop learning, but it does mean their learning is slowed considerably. They still learn when they get a new job or go to new places. But they need to learn much more. And a child should learn everything he or she can.

The reason a child should learn: A child must understand that he himself is the only person on earth who is always going to be with him. A parent, teacher, or policeman is not necessarily going to be there, but you are.

The way a child prepares to act in their best interest is to learn and listen to learn. One way to learn is to read books and newspapers. And a child needs to listen to their parent. A child must understand that when a parent tells them not to do something, it is not because the parent doesn't want the child to have fun.

It is because whatever it is that would be done is harmful for that child in some way or other. Every child should listen to and obey their parents. Parents love their children and would only act in their child's best interest.

Again, I should say that by being older and knowing more than a child, a parent is probably going to know more about a given subject. And we should say that, generally, an older person will probably know more than a younger person. But most certainly by the time people reach the age of about thirty these rules no longer apply. That is because some adults continue to educate themselves and some adults fail to continue to educate themselves. All that brings us back to the question.

Does my being eighty-four years old make me wiser than my seventy-seven-year-old sister? The answer is no! Wisdom is not necessarily always determined by age.

....

In July 2017, I have the same degree of concern about the future of America as I had 60 years ago, when America's policy of defense was MAD (Mutually Assured Destruction). Basically, it meant that if the Soviet Union attacked America with nuclear weapons, we would destroy each other. I thought it extremely irrational.

Today, I find two branches of America's government in crisis, and I should mention that the United States Supreme Court is not one of the two. Officials at the White House seem unable to tell the truth, even when not telling it serves no useful purpose. Our Congress, which has the responsibility to demand the truth, is failing that responsibility.

WE'RE WELL INTO THE SECOND DECADE OF THE TWENTY-FIRST CENTURY

More than two generations have passed since I first started writing these papers. The matters I addressed in some of them have not been resolved to the satisfaction of this author. So, it seems only appropriate to continue discussing and adding other comments to them.

From my perspective, one of the most pressing issues in America today is the way young Black men are losing their lives. We all know that our nation's police sometimes kill them on the slightest pretense. While we all know that one life lost unjustly is one too many, every time it happens we need to know what to do to keep it from happening again. We should insist that every policeman in the nation fully understands that he has no authority to punish any suspected offender. Every officer should be fully reminded of this over and over again throughout his years of duty. And any time a policeman does kill a citizen in the line of duty, there should be an independent board to hold a hearing to determine if the killing was justified.

When there's a determination that the killing was not justified, the evidence should be presented to a grand jury to determine what charges should be made against the policeman. But we know, if we know anything, most young Black men are not being killed by policemen.

By far, most young Black men killed in America are killed by other young Black men. What Black America needs to do, along with stopping all killings of our Black people, is to stop that particular kind of killing, and stop it now. It is in Black communities where Black children learn the difference between right and wrong. We can teach our children, whereas we have little control over what a policeman does.

What do we teach? I have previously mentioned that the responsibility to create the means for this, and to say how it should be done, falls on the shoulders of our leaders and intellectuals, as it seems some parents don't know how to do it themselves.

I'm a layman and address these issues realizing I could be deadly wrong. But I address them freely knowing that someone (including me) has failed to address them adequately.

In the news recently, it was said that fifty-one people were shot over one week or weekend in Chicago. I know there are many people trying to stop this violence, just as I know they are failing miserably.

(Before I go on I should explain that I left school before I graduated from the ninth grade. I got a

GED and about two years of college scattered here and there around the world. I did twenty-three-and-a half years in the U.S. Army and I'm retired from the military.)

So here is my opinion of violence. Violence is contagious, though not necessarily to everyone. Either the psychiatrists don't know it, or have not found cause to say it expressly. Some people observe an act of violence and feel a desire to be a part of it. Add to that the fact that some people have a burning desire to kill someone, just about anyone. Most readers will remember Ted Bundy. But they will not know some of the people I have met.

Prior to going to Vietnam, I worked with a soldier who was a karate expert. He wanted to kill someone by kicking them to death and expressed this desire freely. In 1955, at Beale Air Force Base near Sacramento, I overheard an individual one Sunday morning say he was feeling bad because he hadn't killed anyone since he had left Korea (the Korean War had ended about two years earlier). In Vietnam, I knew a soldier who wanted to kill someone, and I was high on his list. He finally found a way to kill someone and did it pretending it was an accident as he played with a pistol. The Army sent him out to a combat unit rather than punish him.

And just one more story. In Vietnam I had always been curious about the M60 machine guns in each door of our Huey helicopters. One evening I was at our helicopter pad waiting and there sat another copter with the guns in the doors. I asked the crew if I could sit behind one of the guns to see how they felt for firing. I sat there and commented that it was very comfortable. The warrant officer/co-pilot said something to the effect of, "Oh, yes, (naming a previous gunner) killed a lot of Charlies with that gun, but ha, ha, ha, I don't think they were all Charlies." My impression was that he was killing the Vietnam people for the fun of it. And the captain of that helicopter did nothing to discourage it.

Does the contagiousness of violence and the fact that some people like to kill have anything to do with what happened in Chicago on that deadly weekend? I don't know. However, something is happening to make so many people get shot in such a short period of time.

I recall the African boy soldier's comments about how Rambo movies and listening to rap music motivated him to kill people. America's young Black men look at violent video games and listen to rap music, too. Could it be that these games and music are motivating some of them toward violence? I think so and have always thought so. I have read about, and heard of, a certain video game involving stealing cars as being extremely violent. Parents let their children look at this game not knowing that some of them are going to want to do exactly what they see in that game.

So, let us look at four factors in all this violence: violent video games cause some people watching them to want to engage in violence; violence is contagious to some people; most inner-city young Black men grow up listening to rap music and some have access to violent video games; and some people learn to love to kill other people. Any questions? Violent videos and rap music could be major contributors to these problems.

I have found the tone of rap music to be uncompromising. However, I admit I have never liked it at all. Whenever a person listens to music they like, they embrace the philosophy of that music and that has a lot to do with why they like it. If that music is addressing young women as w----- and b------, in the listener's mind that is what they are. As a result, the young men think of them that way and treat them accordingly, causing monumental problems for our young women. The fact that this is happening, and no prominent Black person or organization has publicly condemned it is a national scandal.

....

No discussion of rap music can possibly be made without a discussion of the n-word accompanied by the foulest of language. Neither the n-word nor the foul language would be appropriate at any proper function, such as a college graduation. The deans and professors in their gowns and ribbons would be far too important to hear it. There are many other people in the world that are also too important to hear it, among them my mother, sisters, wife, and daughters. Of course, these purveyors of rap could live another hundred years without thinking of the members of their family in that context. In life, mindset is everything.

Having never been a fan of rap, I can confess to not knowing the words to any rap selections. However, a few years ago I patronized an establishment that hosted a number of different races. To my amazement, the entertainment turned out to be one selection after another of this so called, rap music. And to my dismay, practically every line addressed someone by the n-word, or managed to use the n-word in some context. I was not entertained.

The n-word is a racial slur. Black America considers the word a racial slur when used in any almost context by a non-Black person. When a White talk show host used the word recently referring to himself, there was talk that he should be fired. (I could write a book about the casual way American job holders get fired when everyone knows most adults are in dire need of continuous employment.)

People who think a Black person can use that word publicly, and other people who may not, have gotten simple mindedness down to a science. We live in America. If a Black person may use that word in a song for public consumption, then a person from another race may also use the n-word in a song, generally and politely speaking. But in today's America, it would not be accepted if a White person published a song with the n-word in it, at least not by me and people like me. To clarify, I most certainly do not accept it from Black people either.

I cannot read minds, but I suspect that non-Black people hearing that word in a song probably apply it mentally to any Black person in sight. I got that impression from the White owner of the aforementioned establishment, whose approach to me was about the same he gave to the furniture in his place.

However, in about 1940, a White person did use the n-word in a song at the Grand Ole Opry, as I recall. That was almost eight decades ago, and if I have it right I was about eight years old. I have thought about that event many times since, and I have often imagined what would happen if that singer and I were in such positions that I could push a button and drop him straight off into hell. But I digress.

Surely someone will disagree with me and say they suppose those rap artists made so much money it was worth it. That attitude assumes there is nothing wrong with being a call girl if she makes $5,000 a day. Money is not everything.

—

....

My impression is that people get out of high school, whether they graduate or not, and feel they no longer need to keep educating themselves. It is painful to me to see a group of adults waiting, say to get their vehicle registered, and though they know they are probably going to be there for hours, they are idly staring into space rather than reading. Chances are very good they couldn't name their government representatives, what issues our government has with other nations, or state the temperature at which water freezes. And, of course, they can't recall ever hearing of the aurora borealis or the Kohinoor.

Consequently, when their children ask them questions, there are a great many answers they won't have to give the child. People should attempt to make to some effort to be informed. Uninformed, a person is at the mercy of whatever someone else tells them about any subject they do not know.

One of the things I disagree with, but have heard a lot of, is this: You have got to know where you come from. No! But, people who believe this probably will take up some dress or name that is supposedly connected with their family before slavery. When this happens, I grow concerned that the person is more focused on where they have been than where they are going. I believe that a person who has a good idea of where he or she is going is much better off than a person who simply knows where they came from, although it is great to know both.

We have already discussed the people who followed Jim Jones. They likely believed they knew where they came from. But they didn't know where they were going nor with whom they were going. Consequently, most of them died. Where one is going is not necessarily a geographical location. A person experimenting with cocaine or heroin might be heading to a lifetime of drug dependency. A parent constantly introducing their child as "bad" could be creating depression in that child for a lifetime, a condition that parent will have to contend with for a number of years.

To prevent emotional harm to children, parents must first stop telling their children (who run around screaming at each other) that they are "bad." I've already mentioned this, but saying it again is not a wasted effort. It bears repeating because it is done throughout our society and people simply do not know any better. This is not to suggest that these parents don't love their children as much as any other parent. They simply make the mistake of calling universal childhood activity "bad."

Starting with toddlers, let us teach children a rule to live by. I would say the Golden Rule, but I'm going to invent the Platinum Rule.

THE PLATINUM RULE

We should never do anything to another person that we would not want another person to do to us.

We should have the children repeat this Platinum Rule several times a week and explain exactly what it requires. Adults should realize that the Platinum Rule also applies to them, as they teach it to the children. Imagine what the world would be like if the United Nations could persuade every nation to adopt the Platinum Rule. Practiced across the world, we would have no racism.

But the state of racism in the United States is such that I feel moved to address it here before I go out into the world saying what should be done about it. Before I start, I should say that I can get really upset and out of control about racism. For example, I dropped out of George Washington University, where I worked and attended school, after my American literature class was discussing the Adventures of Huckleberry Finn at the time Roots was showing on TV.

Here is racism in America as I see it:

- Contradictory sentencing practices: The harsh sentences given to crack cocaine users and lighter sentences handed down to those who use the powder form. The number of Black persons jailed for using marijuana, while the states that legalized it reported many more White users than Black. Discussing how the current opioid crisis is killing numerous White people these days, while no one seems to think the answer is to put opioid users in jail. (Not that drug users of any kind should be jailed.)

- Racism of Blacks toward other Blacks: For example, when late in the twentieth century at one very prominent Black university, a dark-skinned Black woman could not be a cheerleader for the sports teams.

- The 2016 presidential election: When Sen. Ted Cruz decided to run for President, it was said, "Yes, he can run. His mother was an American citizen." Yet, from the time Barak Obama began to run for President through his election and eight years as President Barak Obama, no reporter, politician, pundit, or citizen publicly stated that Obama's mother was an American citizen. Apparently, many voters still think he unlawfully held the office. They probably voted for Obama's successor as their hero because for years that successor kept raising questions about Obama's right to hold that office.

- Working class White people concluding they lost their rights: They seemed to blame their problems, such as losing mining jobs, robots replacing humans on assembly lines, and companies moving jobs to India, Indonesia, China, and Pakistan, on having an "unlawfully elected" Black president in office.

Black Lives Matter arose from actions such as a Chicago policeman emptying sixteen rounds into a young Black man who was walking away from him, and a group of New York City police officers choking a man to death as a camera recorded the act. The former remained on duty for a year before being charged, and the latter group was not charged, even though choking was against department policy.

In both instances, crimes more serious than these were committed by public officials who refused to properly prosecute. When organizations such as Black Lives Matter protested they were well within the law. They have made exceedingly good points and have very good reason to exist. But I think we may want to reconsider these protests and acknowledge that we may be witnessing examples of latent racism, when they occur after a relatively small number of Black men are killed by mostly White policemen, and no protests are mounted when several hundred Black men are killed by other Black men.

Something pretty bad has happened in America, but it is not racism. It has to do with manufacturing practices that cost everyone more money and contributes as much, if not more, to the difficulties of making ends meet after a job loss.

I moved to the Atlanta area in 2009 and lived there until 2012. Initially, a certain 16-ounce item in the grocery store cost $2.79. During that time, the item shrunk in size to under ten ounces and went up to $4.49. Another item dropped in size to below 20 ounces. Loaves of bread shrunk by at least two inches or more. A very popular candy bar thinned down, then after some time, thinned again. Jars of some skin care products were made much smaller. About two years ago, I bought a bottle of eye drops that was no bigger than the first joint of my little finger, much smaller than one I had bought a few years earlier. Americans should take note and leave those products on the shelves.

When stores required Americans to give their address and phone number to get a reduced price, customers should have refused. But they didn't. So, here we are toward the end of the second decade of the twenty-first century and our general situation is considerably worse than a decade ago. Our income inequality widens and everything indicates that it will only widen further.

Our two main political parties can no longer address the one out of power as the loyal opposition. They might more appropriately refer to each other as the other contender. White House officials believe in things such as "alternative facts" and make official statements accordingly. It is quite obvious they are not that well-read, or they would realize the dire need for Nineteen Eighty-Four's Ministry of Truth. And some people discussing a certain health care bill in Congress these days seem to need a Ministry of Truth of their very own.

Our government seems to think it more important to make it easier for big companies to make money than to attempt to control global warming. The current government has done little and undone much, which is equal to building nothing and destroying a lot. Politicians boast about being the "party of Lincoln" as they pass laws to try to prohibit citizens in good standing from voting. And if these citizens do vote, they try to negate that vote.

Court rulings suggest these actions are not consistent with what we would have expected from Lincoln but are consistent with what we would have expected from another Civil War era president, Jefferson Davis. Based on what is happening, the United States of America is hardly recognizable. Hopefully those who know Lincoln's values can inform others in the party of just what those values are.

....

Four generations ago, America was in a deep depression. Ordinary families often did not have enough to eat, and those that did have enough had no excess. In most families, everyone followed the clean plate rule, meaning they must eat everything on their plate and under no conditions throw away food that could be safely consumed. Circumstances have changed.

With World War II, people got jobs, they entered the service, and families earned enough money to buy more than enough food at each meal. People also had money to splurge on things like candy and extra snacks. Meanwhile, this rule remained in effect for at least another three generations. With all that food, people still continued to obey the rule. Americans, we should consider changing this rule because we have become overweight.

....

So, there you have it. I had intended to conclude this paper by urging you to save yourselves because the adults are not going to save you.

For the most part, this paper was intended for young Black people. But, with all that's going on in America, I can say it to every young American person: Prepare and save yourselves.

And there is something else I want to say. Somewhere in my papers is a quotation from Andrew Lloyd Webber's Jesus Christ Superstar. Since he has such a way with words, I want to paraphrase him here: America, I never thought we'd come to this.

A TALK ABOUT WAR

We could fill a volume of encyclopedias and not say all there is to be said about war. When I was about four years old, the subject of war came up and my father explained to me that war occurred when men got on a (did he say battle?) field and shot each other. It never occurred to me then that there would be groups on different sides or that my detractors might suggest that I had to go to war (Vietnam) to understand the details.

My intent here is to make certain points of my own and stress that this is just one man's opinion.

My point in bringing up war is that it is so similar to what vulnerable young Black men are experiencing in our urban communities with the prevalence of drug wars and deadly fighting between street gangs. The psychological impact of gang members shooting each other to defend territories and drug sales is just what soldiers experience on the battlefield, only on a smaller scale. But as time has shown, the consequences can be just as great.

It has been said that "war is hell." Anyone who has been in a war probably has no problem agreeing with that. Just as anyone who has been in a war would have a difficult time accepting that someone had been in a "war of words." A real war is when people are in a circumstance to kill or be killed. To a person who has been to war, exchanging unpleasant words with each other is not war. In due time, I expect to get to some very special wars.

Throughout the history of mankind, we have used wars to record time. The Peloponnesian War, the Trojan War, the Hundred Years' War, and so on to the last few centuries. The major wars America has been involved in are: the American Revolutionary War; the War of 1812; the Civil War; the Spanish-American War; World War I; World War II; the Korean War; the Vietnam War; the Gulf War (the First Iraq War); the War in Afghanistan; and the Second Iraq War. Each of these American wars occurred for several reasons, just as wars throughout history around the world occur for a host of reasons. By my casual, layman's observation, it seems that people only need to acquire the weapons and they will create a reason to go to war.

One nation might decide to wage war against another nation because it has something it wants, or it knows the other country cannot adequately defend itself, or both. Examples of nations taking advantage of countries unable to defend themselves against an invader include Germany invading Poland in 1939, Iraq invading Kuwait in 1990, Italy invading Ethiopia in 1935, and Japan invading Manchuria in 1931. One particularly strange war that should be mentioned here is England's opium wars against China in the mid-

84

nineteenth century, which forced China to permit England to sell opium and other products in China.

Then there are the religious wars. First and foremost, among these are the Crusades that Christians fought against Muslims. With limited scholastic experience, there is little I can offer about different religious wars, but I do have something to say about the people who fight them.

My knowledge of religious wars is that they tend to be declared and fought by believers of a religion with only one God. These people often think their particular belief in God makes them somewhat better than someone with a different belief, and especially better than someone who holds no religious beliefs at all. Furthermore, some think their God wants them to convert anyone who believes in another God, or who holds other versions of their own faith. And some believe their God wants them to kill anyone who believes something different than they do.

But they seem to be forgetting something. Believers tend to think of their God as being omnipotent and omnipresent: that He is everywhere at all times and can do anything conceivable just by imagining it. Believers also tend to think that their God, usually a kind and forgiving God, want the non-believers severely punished, or killed, for not believing, and that He would prefer the believers do the punishing than doing it Himself. And while they still believe their God will punish non-believers, they don't fully trust him to do it. Why, I wonder, would they think their God wants something so drastic done to non-believers that He, with all his powers, would not do himself? This kind of thinking puzzles me. But let us get back to war in general.

Wars often start when one nation, or a group of nations, feel they have the weapons and men to go to war. If for some reason a nation doesn't have the weapons, it will not start a war. If a nation goes to war and does not have sufficient military manpower, it will draft its citizens to fight the war. Usually, no consideration is given to whether the men being drafted want to fight the war or not. Their service is demanded. Anyone who attempts to thwart being drafted will be severely punished. Those drafted are required to serve until they are killed, become unable to serve, or their nation determines their services are no longer needed, which is usually when the war has ended.

Wars sometimes end when one belligerent is defeated, or both belligerents conclude that continuing the war is impractical for one reason or another and a truce is negotiated. A truce could be negotiated by the countries fighting the war, or some diplomatically-oriented party or parties not involved in the hostilities may assist in gaining the peace.

In 1905, President Theodore Roosevelt was awarded the Nobel Peace Prize for negotiating peace between Japan and Russia, although America was not involved in that war. It should be mentioned that before peace comes to most wars between major powers, a monumental price is paid by men, and women, on the battlefields and civilians being bombed where the fighting occurs. The number of people adversely affected can range into the millions. Millions of innocent people are sometimes killed, like the Chinese people killed during the Taiping Rebellion or Russians killed during WWII.

Soldiers facing an enemy army on battlefields over an extended period of time, in a kill or be killed situation, may develop severe mental problems. Many will be concerned about staying alive and terribly afraid of dying. Others will be so elated about being in battle they will almost forget to be afraid of dying. All participants' senses will be fully activated. While some will be terribly afraid of dying, especially those in their first battle, others might relish the opportunity to kill someone without legal consequences.

One never knows at what level of insanity another person is functioning. Most people in combat facing an enemy with a machine gun or some other weapon might do anything possible to stay alive. Others will remember that they and their enemy are both human beings and limit their actions accordingly.

Concern about how military people should be treated after they become incapacitated on the battlefield, or in the hands of the enemy, caused twelve nations to convene The Hague, an international court of justice, to establish some rules. In 1864 the nations met. America, probably because of being deeply engaged in the Civil War, was not represented. The new rules determined that once a soldier is no longer a threat to his enemy, they are to be treated humanely and in no way punished in the hands of the enemy unless they misbehave. Over the next century, nations met a number of times, in 1899, 1906, and 1928, to add rules about the treatment of civilians. More rules were added between 1949 to 1972. These meetings continuously improved the treatment of people during wars or any circumstance where one country has control over, or occupies another, country. These rules became known as the Geneva Conventions, and at one time they had been signed by one hundred and ninety-six countries. Over the years, some countries have deliberately violated the conventions, even after agreeing to obey them.

Japan's violation: In 1931 Japan invaded China through Manchuria. Despite being inside China, Japan somehow avoided any major battles with the Chinese army until the summer of 1937. Japan's Emperor Hirohito was persuaded by the Imperial Japanese Army to sign an order, on Aug. 5, 1937, that allowed its army to disregard the rules of the Geneva

Conventions in China. Why would they do a thing like that?

Four days after the Emperor signed the order, Japanese officials in China staged the Battle of Shanghai, the first major battle between Japan and China in that war (some historians consider this battle the start of World War II).

China fought gallantly at Shanghai but lost several battles in and around the city. After winning at Shanghai, Japan's Imperial Army headed toward Nanjing, China's capital, fighting China's army along the way. Nanjing tried to defend itself but was defeated in the first two weeks. Immediately after that defeat began "The Rape of Nanjing," a series of mass murders and rapes.

Rape may be the far lesser offense committed by the Japanese military in Nanjing. Japanese soldiers would go into a house, and sometimes they would kill the men and rape the women, then kill the women, too. Other times, they would enter a building and round up a group of women, and several soldiers would rape the women then kill them all. When Chinese soldiers surrendered, Japanese soldiers would line them up and shoot them. Two junior Japanese officers held a contest — who could be the first to kill a hundred Chinese with a sword. When both exceeded a hundred and they couldn't determine who had won, they started over again, this time raising the goal to one hundred and fifty (after the war those two Japanese officers were hanged). Japanese soldiers were also accused of forcing family members to commit incest, making boys have sex with their sisters and their mother. These atrocities continued for about a month until a Japanese general stopped it. A Japanese prince who was in charge of the Japanese forces in China could have put a stop to it. But he did not. Some Japanese military personnel were tried and hanged for their actions in Nanjing, but the prince was spared.

Like Shanghai, Nanjing had a large international community. Some of the foreigners tried to stop the Japanese soldiers from committing these atrocities. One foreigner in particular is credited with saving about two-hundred-thousand Chinese lives. This foreigner was a Nazi. Altogether, the number of Chinese murdered at Nanjing is estimated at roughly three hundred thousand. In the years since 1937, some Japanese politicians and citizens have denied the Rape of Nanjing. However, many others have verified it, including Chinese citizens, foreign businessmen, foreign journalists, missionaries, diplomats, foreign priests, Chinese soldiers, and Japanese soldiers.

America, too, has been known to violate the Geneva Conventions. To America's credit, the violations have not been condoned by our government, and America is not denying to the rest of the world that they happened.

MY LAI

My Lai is a village in South Vietnam. The name also refers to a horrific incident that occurred there in 1968.

More than five hundred villagers were killed, about two-thirds of them women and children. American soldiers shot the villagers, set their huts on fire and raped many of the women before killing them. One soldier is alleged to have commanded four women to strip naked, so he could rape them. They stripped, but when they resisted the rape, he killed them all. Some soldiers killed women and the babies they held in their arms. One soldier shot himself in the foot to avoid taking part in the massacre, while others refused outright. The massacre continued for several hours, until a helicopter pilot flying overhead saw what was happening. He landed the helicopter and got between some soldiers and their intended victims, saving the village from further slaughter.

When soldiers who witnessed the slaughter My Lai reported it up the chain of command in Vietnam, their reports were ignored. Consequently, the American public did not learn about My Lai until sometime the next year, in 1969.

Of the fourteen men initially charged in the massacre, only one of them was convicted. Lt. William Calley was sentenced to life in prison. Shortly after his conviction, he was released from prison and placed in house arrest. After three-and-a-half years, he was paroled. Many Americans complained that he was tried at all.

Since American officials knew what had happened and failed to hold the soldiers accountable, we cannot say we behaved any better than the Japanese who deny the Rape of Nanjing.

The Rape of Nanjing and the My Lai Massacre are examples of what men do in wars when they attain total power. The saying that "power corrupts, and absolute power corrupts absolutely" has raised its ugly head. Sometimes people find themselves in circumstances where they can do awful things to others, and they take advantage of that and believe they will never be held accountable. All too often, they are not held accountable. The Nuremberg Trials and Tokyo Trials are rare exceptions.

A STORY

In 1962, as a staff sergeant in the United States Air Force, I was assigned to Taiwan. Formerly known as Formosa, Taiwan is a Chinese Island that was ceded to Japan in 1895 after Japan defeated China, but was then ceded back to China after the Japanese defeat in WWII. Chiang Kai-shek moved the government of China to Taiwan after his Kuomintang army was defeated and driven from the Chinese mainland in 1949. My story here mostly concerns the time the island was in the hands of the Japanese government.

My position in Tainan, Taiwan was flight commander in the Air Police (Air Force Military Police). I supervised about forty men. One day, one of my police patrols brought a Chinese man to me who had a contraction strapped to his back. The Chinese man's supervisor, also Chinese, soon arrived. I talked to them, as we were in their country and they deserved that respect. I released the worker.

It turned out the Chinese supervisor was a martial arts specialist and had been training some of my subordinates. He had told them he would like to meet me.

He told me his name, Nagasaki, and that he was thirty years old, my age. Actually, he was a year younger because Chinese people believe a person is a year old when they are born. He told me he was a civil engineer working on a project at the Tainan Air Force Base, where I was stationed. He had once been a pilot for a kamikaze submarine in the Japanese Navy, which is little more than a torpedo with a pilot whose intent is to drive the little submarine into a ship and blow up the ship and himself. In 1945, Nagasaki was fully deployed with three other submarines in the bay near the Philippine Islands with a fleet of American ships anchored before them. As they approached the

American ships intent on blowing themselves up, word came over the radio that the war was over. He, his fellow pilots, and the Americans were saved. Nagasaki was thirteen years old. His leader was seventeen years old and would later become a co-founder of the Sony Corporation. Nagasaki explained to me his idea of why the Japanese military would want a twelve or thirteen-year old to be a kamikaze. Twenty-year-old men would have enough life experience and appreciation to change their minds about dying for the emperor. Children his age were easily indoctrinated, and there was little probability they would change their minds about blowing themselves up for the emperor.

But now back to war. In America, over the years, we have talked about the drug wars between our young men in our cities. I have never known myself to be in contact with any drug gang member. I had always imagined myself telling a drug gang member that, "war is not one of your options." But, had I done so, I would have been dreadfully wrong. Those children are at least as much at war as I was in Vietnam, and possibly more so. I have many reasons for believing this.

Too many times, I have read about or heard some young person interviewed on TV saying they do not expect to live to be twenty years old. In some neighborhoods, every person over ten years old knows someone who was murdered, probably by gunshot. Everyone knows there are gangs in some neighborhoods. And everyone knows that each gang considers itself the owner of certain areas. They believe this ownership authorizes them to kill any member of another gang who enters their territory. What they probably do not know is that this is one of the same standards held by the Ku Klux Klan.

In America however, a citizen does not need the permission of another citizen to walk a city street in any given area. As Americans, gang leaders should behave accordingly and avoid wars. Gang wars involve shoot-outs. When one gang member is shooting at another, he has no concern about hitting an innocent bystander. There are no rules like the Geneva Conventions. "Convention? What is a convention? And who the hell thinks we need one? What we need is to get those .... over there dead." These shooters probably do not recognize the term. To them, any one they kill unintentionally is just "collateral damage" who had the bad luck to be in the wrong place at the wrong time.

Like nations, if a gang wants a young man or young woman to become a member – they are not asked to join, they are told to join. In other words, the member is drafted in the same way that armies are built. If someone refuses to join, there are dire consequences. That person might be seriously beaten or killed. It is true that some children might want to join a gang. If a fourteen-year-old is being bullied by someone, or if he sees gang members as the most affluent members of society, he might find gang membership acceptable.

Once in a gang, however it comes about, the new member must do what he is ordered to do, just like an army soldier. New members probably rank high on the "hit list" of other gangs. Gang leaders will probably give the new member a gun at the earliest opportunity and urge him to use it unlawfully. That way, the new member will have reason to stay in the gang. New gang members might love the power of having a gun and the ability to take a life in a gang war.

Gangs will probably always be around. Most likely, their leaders have never heard of diplomacy. If they have heard of it, it is doubtful they have ever considered applying it to their circumstances. Anyone inclined to negotiate a peace between the gangs probably would not know who the gang leaders are.

So, gangs are at war. The psychological effect on young gang members in our communities is very close to what soldiers in shooting wars between nations experience. Young people are very susceptible to the influence, or indoctrination, of their elders. Just as Nagasaki was persuaded to give his life for Japan and its Emperor, young gang members are persuaded to commit any crime their leaders ask of them. In general, war is evil and so is gang war.

Drug wars are not America's first gang wars. During prohibition, people distributing alcoholic beverages also had wars. One of them was the Saint Valentine's Day Massacre, a 1929 gang murder that killed seven men in Chicago. We can see that civilian gangs are capable of the same kinds of cruelties that occurred at Nanjing and My Lai, if only on a smaller scale.

Families, communities and governments must ensure that our children are not forced to join gangs. If it means parents having to walk their children to and from school, so be it. Children must be protected from being drafted into gangs. Children should be told at every age about the perils of being in a gang. All adults, families, communities and governments should realize that children learn what is presented to them. If parents and teachers don't teach them, someone else will. We should ensure that children know that being in a gang probably means being in gang wars. While many children are not gang members, one child in a gang is one too many. Everyone should ensure that our children are protected first and educated second.

This is where the Platinum Rule comes in. We should make every effort to ensure our children feel safe, think smart, and lookout for others.

A generation ago, America had a great first lady who told us that *"It takes a village"*. In very recent years, America had another great first lady who gave this standard to America *"When they go low, we go high."* These invaluable rules should be understood and employed by us all, and while we are out doing things, let us go back a half century and take a page out of the book of non-other than Chairman Mao, himself, and *"LET A HUNDRED FLOWERS BLOOM."*

Made in United States
North Haven, CT
27 April 2022